The Little
Gardeners
Guide

Niki
Horin

Alicat

Contents

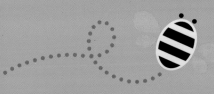

Grow it and gobble it! 38

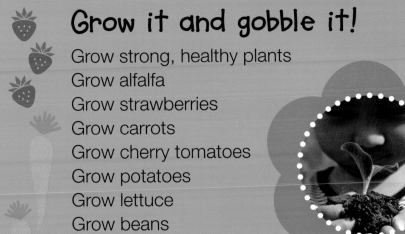

Make-and-do gardening fun! 50

How to be a little gardener

Gardening is all about growing and caring for plants. You don't even need to have a garden. Plants can grow in any container.

Gardening can be dirty fun so you will need to have some special clothes to get started.

Little gardener clothes

A hat—for shade from the sun

SUNCREEN LOTION

Lots of sunscreen lotion—so you don't get sunburned

Sunglasses—because it's bright out in the sun

Gloves—to keep your hands clean

Rain boots— to keep your feet warm and dry

Little gardener tools

Gardening fork—to loosen soil

Rake—to smooth the soil

Trowel—to dig holes

A **wheelbarrow** or **pull wagon**—to carry big loads

Watering can—to water your plants

Bucket—to carry your weeds and garbage

Be safe!

Gardening is really fun but remember:

- Use child-sized gardening tools, which fit nicely in little hands

- Tools are sharp, so make sure a grown-up is there to help

- At the end of the day, put your tools away, because they will rust when left outside

Are you ready for some fun Little Gardener? Jump into your rain boots, and let's head out into the garden!

Be a garden explorer!

Your garden is an exciting place just waiting for you to discover its secrets! Although it looks quiet out there, your garden really is a very busy place.

Plants are growing, and insects and little animals are busy with their day's activities.

There is just so much to explore.
Let's get out there and see
what we can find!

What's in the garden?

Gardens are full of amazing things! There are lots of plants and animals.

Some are so small that they are hard to see, but they all live happily together.

Water

Every living thing needs water. It comes from the sky as rain, hail, or snow!

Plants can grow in all sorts of pots—inside and outside.

Plants

Plants are living things that are grown in the garden. They can grow to be huge like a tree or stay tiny like grass.

Splashing in rain puddles is fun to do!

Plants are our food!

Mother bird

Baby birds calling for their lunch

Bird nests are built high up in trees

Bird nests are made from sticks, leaves, hair, and bird spit!

Animals and their homes

Many animals make their homes in gardens. Worms live under the soil. Spiders and ants live on top of the soil.

Bugs live on plant leaves. Birds and bees live in trees and bushes.

Soil

Soil is the top layer of the ground, like icing on a birthday cake! It's made up of rocks, dead leaves, plant roots, dead bugs, and stuff like that.

What are plants?

Plants are living things just like us, except they grow in soil.

We can't see their roots, which are under the soil, but we can see their stems and leaves.

Plants can look very different from each other, but amazingly they all have a stem, roots, and leaves.

All plants have:
- a stem
- leaves
- roots

What the stem, leaves and roots look like depends on what type of plant you are looking at.

Some plants have flowers

Stem

Leaves

Roots

What do plants do?

Plants give us all the things we need to live. They also keep the air fresh and are homes for animals.

Plants as animal homes

Animals of all sizes—from large to teeny tiny—live on plants and trees. Orangutans, birds, bugs, and beetles can all live together on plants.

Plants as food

Plants are food for all living things. Lots of animals, like cows, eat grass and seeds, while other animals and people eat fruit, seeds, and vegetables.

Plants clean the air

All living things need to breathe clean air. Plants keep the air we breathe stocked full of oxygen.

We also get medicine, clothes, and paper from plants.

Types of plants

There are millions of different types of plants. To make it easy, we can think of them in groups of plants that look the same.

Trees

Trees are the world's largest plants! The stem of a tree is called a trunk and is made of wood.

Grasses

Grasses are plants with long, thin leaves. Lots of grass makes lawn.

All these fruit and vegetables come from plants.

Fruit and vegetables

Fruit and vegetables are parts of a plant that we eat.

Flowers

Some plants grow flowers with beautiful petals.

Succulents

Some plants store water. These are called succulents (say suk-u-lents) like cactus plants. Watch out for their sharp needles!

Ferns

Ferns are lovely soft, green plants with pretty leaves called fronds.

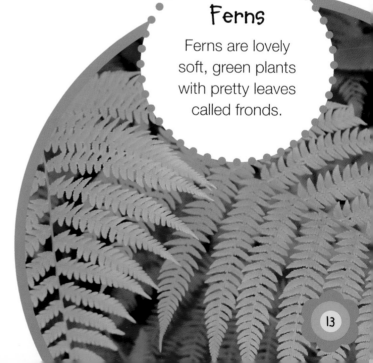

Where do plants come from?

Have fun finding seeds in your food or use parts of other plants to grow new ones!

Most new plants grow from the seeds or spores that grow inside other plants. Some start from parts of other plants.

Plants from seeds

Many grasses, trees, and flowering plants grow from seeds. Seeds can come in all different shapes and sizes.

Pumpkin seeds

Avocado seed

Tomato seeds

Plants from spores

Some mosses, ferns, and funguses grow from spores.

Millions of spores grow in spore cases under a fern's fronds, or leaves.

Plants from cuttings

New plants can also grow from cut-off parts of other plants. A new strawberry plant can grow from a strawberry vine or runner.

A new cactus can grow from another cactus.

From flower to fruit

We get our fruit from flowers that have been pollinated. This is when pollen from a plant goes to another of the same kind. Then the flower dies and a new fruit with seeds grows in its place.

An apple tree grows flowers. These flowers are pollinated.

Then the flower dies and fruit begins to grow.

The seeds of an apple tree are in the fruit.

The pollinators

Some flowering plants can pollinate alone. Others need animals to carry their pollen to another plant. Lots of animals help pollinate plants, but the best are bees! When a bee visits flowers, pollen sticks to its hairy legs. Some of the pollen falls off on the next flower it visits. The wind carries seeds and spores to new places, too!

Bees visit flowers and pollinate them!

How do plants eat?

Plants don't have mouths, so they can't eat like us. Instead they need water, soil, air, and sunlight to make food inside their special plant parts. This is called photosynthesis (say fotto-sin-the-sus).

The plant food recipe

Photosynthesis is just a big word for how plants make food. The main parts are water, soil, and air. The sun gives the energy needed to mix them together.

Water
Plants need water, too! They use rain or a sprinkle from your watering can. The soil soaks up the water.

Soil
Soil is full of good stuff that keeps plants healthy. The plant uses its roots like a straw to drink nutrients and water from the soil.

Air
The sky is filled with air. Air has a gas called carbon dioxide. The plant's leaves breathe it in and use the carbon to make food. They breathe out the oxygen.

Sunlight
The sun gives plants lots of energy to mix the parts it needs from the soil, water, and air to make plant food.

Photosynthesis is how a plant mixes parts of the air and soil. It gets help from the sunlight to make food.

The sun's energy comes to Earth as heat and light.

Water soaks into the soil.

The plant breathes in air through its leaves.

The plant's leaves soak up the sunlight and use it to mix all the parts of the plant food.

The plant drinks nutrients from soil.

How do seeds grow into plants?

Seedlings are baby plants. A seed can grow into a seedling in as little as a week. It just needs good soil, water, and sun.

From seed to seedling in four steps!

1. The seed is planted in airy soil. The seed has all the food that it needs to grow.

2. If there is enough water, air, and heat in the soil, a plant shoot will soon grow up toward the warm sun.

What if plants didn't have water or sun? Plants need air, soil, water, and sun to grow. If not, they can't live!

First leaves are called "seed" leaves. They look different from the later leaves of a plant.

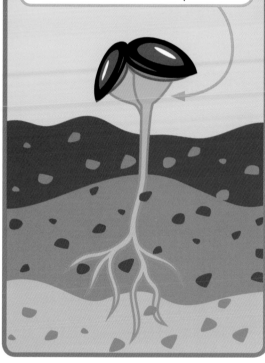

3 As the seed pushes through the soil, its seed coat falls off and its first leaves appear. Now the plant can make its own food through photosynthesis. Soon it has a stem and roots, too!

4 Soon after the "seed" leaves have grown, the first real leaves of the plant will appear. With good care, this little seedling will grow flowers and fruit!

What animals are in the garden?

All kinds of animals live in gardens. Some are good, but others can make trouble when they feed on plants' roots, fruit, leaves, and juices. Help your garden by knowing which animals are good and which animals are really naughty!

The good ones!

Bees

Bees help flowers grow fruit, and they make honey! But stay away from them so you don't get stung!

Worms

Gardeners love worms! Worms eat soil and when it comes out the other end, it has more nutrients. This is great for your plants. Worms are so helpful that gardeners sometimes build worm farms.

To learn how to build a worm farm, see pages 58 and 59.

Frogs

If you are lucky
and have a pond,
you might also have frogs.
Frogs help by eating lots of
plant-feeding bugs before they
gobble up your plants!

Dragonflies

Dragonflies are bugs that have
been around since the days
of the dinosaurs! They can
catch plant-feeding bugs
while flying in the air!

21

Butterflies

Butterflies are beautiful garden friends. And they help pollinate flowers, too!

Praying mantis

Praying mantises are the coolest-looking insects! They blend in with the garden and eat plant-eating bugs like aphids and beetles.

Birds

Most birds help gardens by eating plant-feeding bugs in the garden like snails and slugs. But birds snack on fruit and seedlings, too. A scarecrow can help keep the birds away.

To make your own scarecrow, see page 57.

Ladybugs

Ladybugs help gardens because they eat aphids and other plant-feeding insects. But look out for the 28-spotted ladybug that likes to munch on leaves. Always count the spots!

Spiders

Spiders also help by gobbling plant-feeding insects. Spiders live in webs, under rocks, or in leaf piles. Always keep away from spiders because some bite if they are scared.

Centipedes

Centipedes hunt naughty bugs like slugs and snails. But centipedes can bite, so leave them alone to do their good work in the garden.

23

The naughty ones!

Naughty garden animals eat leaves and fruit, suck juices from plants, and chew on the roots. You may find a few of these in your garden. But don't let too many move in!

Aphids

Aphids are tiny bugs that suck the juices out of plants. They really like roses and citrus trees. Ladybugs can eat lots of aphids. If you don't have ladybugs, wash the aphids off your plants with water.

Snails and slugs

Snails and slugs are sneaky night gobblers that eat new leaves on plants. Sprinkle sawdust or eggshells around your seedlings to keep them away.

Fruit flies

Female fruit flies damage fruit by "stinging" their eggs into apples, pears, and other fruit. Their babies grow inside the fruit and feed on it, so the fruit goes bad on the tree. Keep your fruit safe by covering it with a paper bag.

Caterpillars

Caterpillars are the chubby babies of moths and butterflies. These bright wrigglers have sharp mouths and are fast at munching leaves and roots. Be sure to pick them off your plants. But always use gloves! The hairs on their bodies can give a bad sting!

Stinkbugs

Stinkbugs suck the juice from fruit, like oranges and lemons. There are many types and most are very large. You can stop them by moving them. But always use gloves and wear sunglasses. Stinkbugs spray a stink liquid when they are scared. It can sting if it gets in your eyes!

Are you ready to start planting, Little Gardener? Grab your tools and get started!

Get into gardening!

By now you know that plants need soil, air, and light to make their food. But like family pets, plants need more than food to be healthy and happy. They need YOU! You need to do a lot of things to help your plants as they grow. It is a lot of work, but it's fun to create your very own garden.

Let's get those plants growing!

Planning your garden

Plants can grow almost anywhere! Use a pot if you don't have a garden. Even if you do have a garden, plant all your seeds in pots first. You can move seedlings into the garden plot later on.

Getting your garden plot ready

You will need to do some work to prepare the garden plot for your plants.

To make your own compost, see pages 58, 59, and 60.

Clearing the plot

You will need to pull out all the weeds.

Next use your gardening fork to loosen and add air to the soil.

Check your soil

What kind of soil do you have? Is it sandy or clay?

Sandy has a lot of rough pieces and clay has teeny tiny pieces. Sandy soil helps the water go through the soil.

A garden plot has lots of room to grow!

Picking your pots

If you want to grow your plants in pots, you need to find some first.

Be sure to get big ones, too, for when your plants grow larger.

Collecting pots

You will need many pots in lots of different sizes. But you don't have to go to the store. First, ask your family and friends if they have any extra pots or baskets.

Next look around the house for different containers like small tubs, plastic bottles, or even a shoe or an old toy truck for larger plants. Try to find fun containers for a great garden!

Getting the pots ready

Once you have your pots and containers, follow these steps:

1. Clean all your pots and containers.

2. Now it's time to decorate them!

3. Next **ask an adult** to help punch some holes in the bottom of the pots.

   These holes let out any extra water.

4. Cover the holes with stones, so the water won't run out the bottom when you water your plants.

5. Fill your pots with rich compost (food and garden waste) or potting mix.

To paint your pots and containers, see page 52.

29

A tiny seedling sprouting from the soil

Growing plants from seeds

To grow your plants from seeds, plant them in small indoor pots. This will keep them safe from bad weather and hungry snails, slugs, and caterpillars.

To grow strong, healthy plants, see pages 40 and 41.

1 Find a small pot that has holes in the bottom and fill it with soil. Push your finger halfway into the soil to make a small hole.

2 Add two seeds into the hole and gently cover it with soil. Give it a little water and place the pot on a windowsill.

3 When the seeds grow, take out the smaller seedling to give the strongest seedling room to grow.

4 When it's time to move to a bigger pot, gently take it out with its soil. When you pot it again, put the soil back.

5 How much water you give your plant depends on its type.

6 Follow the directions on the seed packet to care for your new plant.

Protecting your plants

You'll want to keep your plants safe from animals and bad weather.

In pots

Keeping plants in pots safe is easy. Move them high up away from hungry animals. Or put them inside when the weather is bad.

Caterpillars, slugs, and snails like to gobble plants!

In a garden plot

Plant-eating animals and bad weather can hurt garden plants. You can't move plants in a plot, but you can build something to keep the bad things out.

1. Find a clear plastic drink bottle that is larger than your plant.

2. **Ask an adult** to cut off the top of the bottle and make a hole at the bottom of the bottle.

3. Put the bottle over the top of your plant. Be careful not to crush the stem or leaves.

4. Push the bottle well into the soil.

Now your plant is super safe! Do these steps for every plant in your plot.

Cover new fruit with netting or a paper bag, so birds won't eat it for dinner!

For more about plant-eating animals, see pages 24 and 25.

Watering your plants

Your plants need water in the morning, but not every day. Instead, they need a lot of water every few days. Always point your watering can at the soil, not the plant! Watering on the plant can hurt its newest parts.

Weeding your plants

Weeds are plants that you didn't plant, and you really don't want them! Weeds grow fast, and they can keep your plants from growing. Pull them up by their roots or use your trowel. Plant labels will help you know which plants aren't weeds!

Always use a watering can. It will help keep you from giving your plants too much water.

To make plant labels, see pages 54 and 55.

Mulching your plants

Mulch is a layer on top of the soil, which keeps your plants warm, stops weeds from growing, and the soil from getting too dry. Be sure to add mulch after weeding and watering your plants.

Thinning your plants

As they grow bigger, your plants will need more room to grow. If your seedlings or plants look too close to each other, it's time to move some to another pot or a different part of your plot. This is called thinning. Only throw away the smallest, weakest plants.

Thinning your plants
gives them room to grow!

Supporting your plants

Some plants that are really tall or have lots of fruit need help standing up. You can do this with stakes or trellises.

Stake

A stake can be a bamboo pole or a sturdy stick.

To use a stake:

1. **Ask an adult** to stick the stake into the soil next to your plant. Be sure not to hurt the roots.

   The best time to add a stake is when the plant is small.

2. Gently tie the stem of the plant to the stake with string.

3. As your plant grows, tie the new growth to the stake, too!

TOMATO
Grosse Lisse

Always **ask an adult** to help with stakes and trellises, and keep your eyes away from the ends. They are sharp and pointy!

Trellis

A trellis helps climbing roses and other vines to stand. A trellis is often put on a fence, but it can also be stuck in a pot or garden plot.

To use a trellis:

1. **Ask an adult** to tie the trellis to a fence or to push it into the soil.

2. To put your plant on the trellis, wrap the stem on the "Xs" of the trellis.

3. As your plant grows, help it go up the trellis by adding new growth to the "Xs."

Are you ready to grow some fruit and veggies, Little Gardener? It will soon be time to collect your basket and pick some fun food!

Grow it and gobble it!

Now you know a lot about gardens and how to care for them. So it's time to grow your own plants! And the best plants to grow are the ones you can gobble!

Just follow the next steps and soon you'll have fresh fruit and veggies at home!

39

Grow strong, healthy plants

For your seeds to grow strong and healthy, they need the right care. Each type of plant needs different things. Finding out what works is part of the fun of gardening!

Why plants sometimes don't grow

Plants may not grow because:

- they aren't the right type for where you live
- they are planted at the wrong time of year
- they are hurt by weather or animals
- they are underwatered or overwatered
- they get too much or not enough sun

For more information about
- how to prepare pots for plants, see page 29
- how to grow plants from seeds, see pages 30 and 31.

Plant-growing tips

The right care

Seed packets and seedling labels can tell you a lot about the care a plant needs to grow healthy and strong, like how much water or sun to give it.

Don't forget to water your plants!

The right type of soil

Fruit and vegetable plants grow best in light soil that crumbles. If the soil isn't right in your garden, you can add liquid plant food or compost. Or you can grow your plants in pots and use potting mix.

Shelter your plants

Plants should be grown in a covered spot. This will keep them from getting hurt by storms, wind, cold, or too much rain.

The right sunlight

All plants need sunlight, but some need more than others. Be sure to check the seed packet to find out how much yours need.

Grow alfalfa

Alfalfa sprouts are fast and easy to grow. They don't need sunlight, soil, or pots!

You will need:

- A handful of alfalfa seeds
- A glass jar with a heavy bottom and a wide top
- A piece of muslin (plain cotton fabric)
- A rubber band
- Water

When to plant:

Any time of year

Sunlight:

No sun needed. Grow in a warm, dark place, like inside a cabinet

Watering:

Twice a day (see steps 3 and 5)

Protect them from:

No protection needed

How long until you see an alfalfa sprout?

Within 1 week

What to do:

1   Put all the seeds into the glass jar.

2   Cover the top of the jar with the muslin. **Ask an adult** to put a rubber band around the top of the jar to hold the fabric in place.

3   Pour water through the muslin, until the jar is half full. Now carefully turn the jar upside down. Hold the muslin in place and pour out the water.

4   Put the jar in a warm, dark place.

5   Twice a day wet the seeds like you did in step 3.

6   When your sprouts have grown, wash them well before eating them.

How to gobble alfalfa!

Try some alfalfa on a sandwich for some extra crunch!

Alfalfa sprouts are a super-easy food to grow!

Grow strawberries

You can grow strawberry plants from cuttings called "runners." The best way to grow them is in hanging baskets. Let them grow wild!

What to do:

1. Use the cardboard to cover the inside of the hanging basket.

2. Add soil to the basket.

3. Water the soil until it is all wet.

4. Make some small holes in the soil and plant the roots of each strawberry runner. Cover with soil and water it well.

5. Hang the basket in a sunny, covered spot.

6. Weed your hanging basket often.

How to gobble strawberries!
Strawberries are so yummy cut up on top of pancakes!

You will need:
- A hanging basket
- Potting mix
- Cardboard
- 6 strawberry runners
- Water

When to plant:
Winter

Sunlight:
Full sun—at least 6 hours of sun a day

Watering:
Water once or twice a week

Protect them from:
Birds, snails, and slugs

How long until you see a strawberry?
About 2 months

The redder the strawberry, the sweeter it will be!

Grow carrots

Carrots are the roots of the plant that grow under the ground. You will know they are growing when you see the tops peek out of the soil!

You will need:

- A pencil
- Carrot seeds
- A large, deep pot
- Potting mix
- Water

When to plant:

Early to mid-spring

Sunlight:

A shaded spot is OK, but it needs full sun for some of the day

Watering:

Keep well watered

Protect them from:

Carrot flies

How long until you see a carrot?

About 3 months

What to do:

1. Use a pencil to press a line into the soil.

2. Sprinkle seeds on the line and cover them with a little soil.

3. Press the soil down and water gently.

4. Water your plants well for 7 to 10 days, until seedlings pop up.

5. If the seedlings are too close, pull the weak ones out. The plants should be one hand's length apart (from your wrist to the tip of your finger).

6. When the stalks are two hand lengths tall, pull one out to see how the carrots are growing. Keep checking until they are ready.

How to gobble carrots!

Carrots are delicious right after you pick them. Just don't forget to wash off the dirt!

Baby carrots are sweeter than big carrots.

Grow cherry tomatoes

Cherry tomatoes are yummy tiny tomatoes. Be sure to use a stake to help them stand up.

What to do:

1. Dig a hole in the soil.

2. Gently place the seedling in the hole.

3. Press the soil by the roots and water it well.

4. **Ask an adult** to put the stake into the soil, but not near the plant's roots. As your plant grows tall, gently tie it to the stake.

5. Add straw or compost.

6. Keep your plant in a sunny spot.

7. You'll know it's time to pick when your plant has round, red tomatoes!

How to gobble cherry tomatoes!

Add these cherry tomatoes to your salads, pizzas, or pasta sauce!

Tomatoes are ripe when they're red!

You will need:
- A medium-size pot
- Potting mix
- A tomato seedling
- A stake
- String
- Water

When to plant:

Mid-spring to mid-summer

Sunlight:

Full sun—at least 6 hours of sun a day

Watering:

2 to 3 times a week

Protect them from:

Caterpillars and aphids

How long until you see a tomato?

About 3 months

Grow potatoes

Potatoes grow underground.
You only need one potato to grow
lots of them!

You will need:

- A potato that is beginning to sprout
- A bucket or a bin, with holes at the bottom for drainage
- Potting mix
- Water

When to plant:

At any warm time of the year

Sunlight:

Full sun—at least 6 hours of sun a day

Watering:

Water often to keep soil moist

Protect them from:

Beetles

How long until you see a potato?

About 4 months

What to do:

1 Fill container a little less than half with soil.

2 Put the potato on top and then cover with soil.

3 Water well.

4 As the plant grows, add more potting mix, so the stem is always covered.

5 After the plant has flowers, you may see "fruit." Don't eat these. They are poison.

6 After it flowers, the plant will start to die. Now it's time to tip over the container and count your potatoes!

How to gobble potatoes!

You can eat potatoes so many ways. Mashed, baked, or French fries... Yum!

Never eat uncooked or green potatoes. You can get very sick!

Grow lettuce

You can grow lettuce in pots, but be sure to give each plant lots of room to grow.

What to do:

1 Use a pencil to press a line into the soil.

2 Sprinkle seeds on the line and cover them with a little soil.

3 Press the soil down and water well.

4 When the seedlings appear, gently move each plant to its own pot and water well.

5 Add gravel or shells to cover the layer of soil for each plant.

6 When the leaves are large, they are ready to eat. Pick them off as you need them. The plant will grow more.

7 When the plant grows a big, thick stalk in the center, it's time to grow new lettuce.

How to gobble lettuce!
Be sure to wash your lettuce well. Then add it to a sandwich!

You will need:
- A medium-size pot to grow seedlings
- Potting mix
- Pencil
- Lettuce seeds
- Water

When to plant:
Spring and summer

Sunlight:
A shaded spot is OK, but it needs full sun for some of the day

Watering:
Water every day to keep the soil wet

Protect them from:
Snails, slugs, and caterpillars

How long until you see lettuce?
About 2 to 3 months

There are lots of types of lettuce!

Grow beans

Growing your very own curvy, bendy, monster-size beanstalk is lots of fun… just don't try to climb it!

You will need:

- 4 bean seeds
- A big pot
- 4 stakes
- Potting mix
- String
- Water

When to plant:

Early spring

Sunlight:

A shaded spot is OK, but it needs full sun for some of the day.

Watering:

Water daily to keep soil moist

Protect them from:

Slugs

How long until you see a bean?

Around 3 to 5 months

What to do:

1 **Ask an adult** to push the 4 stakes (about 3 hands' length apart) into the soil. Tie them at the top of the string, like a tepee.

2 Put a bean seed next to each stake and push the seed a finger deep into the soil.

3 Cover seeds and water well.

4 As the plants grow, wrap the stem of each plant around its stake.

5 When you see flowers, you'll have beans soon. Pick them when they are young. The more beans you pick, the more they will grow.

How to gobble beans!

There are so many kinds of beans, and they are good in soups!

Beans come in many shapes and sizes!

48

Grow lemons

It can take 8 years to grow a lemon tree from a seed! So let's start with a baby lemon tree.

What to do:

1. Fill your pot with special potting mix for lemon plants.

2. Make a hole in the soil that is twice as deep as the plant's roots.

3. **Ask an adult** to help you move the plant from its old pot to your new pot.

4. Gently fill soil around the plant.

5. Now water the plant well. This is very important because it helps to pack the soil tightly against the roots of the tree.

6. Add some soft mulch on top of the soil.

7. Your tree will grow flowers in the springtime. Once pollinated, the plant will grow fruit.

How to gobble lemons!
Mix your lemon juice with sugar and water for your own lemonade!

You can pick your lemons when they are all yellow.

You will need:
- A young lemon tree plant
- Citrus potting mix
- Huge pot
- Water
- Soft mulch

When to plant:
Any time of year, but avoid moving plants when they are flowering or fruiting

Sunlight:
Full sun—at least 6 hours of sun a day

Watering:
After watered in, not often, only water when the topsoil is dry

Protect them from:
Fruit flies and other insects

How long until you see a lemon?
Most likely in spring

49

Ok Little Gardener, it's time to get busy making and doing!

Sophie's scallions

50

Make-and-do gardening fun!

Being a little gardener is not just about growing plants. It's also about making the garden a special place of your very own!

The fun make-and-do projects on the next pages will keep you busy, even when you're not in the garden!

Paint your own pots

Painting your own pots and containers is a great way to add color to your garden. You can paint lots of crazy patterns or cool pictures!

You will need:

- A place to paint (**ask an adult** where you can paint)
- Painting smock, or old clothes
- Pots and containers
- Childrens paints (nontoxic)
- Paintbrushes of different sizes
- Jar with water to clean your paintbrushes
- Old newspaper

What to do:

1. After you set up your paints, carefully paint a pattern or picture on a pot.

2. When you have finished, let your pot dry.

3. Be sure to keep your wet pot in a place out of reach where it won't be touched.

4. When the pot is dry, it will be a bright new home for a plant!

Write WET PAINT on the newspaper under your wet pot, so no one will touch it.

Make your own decorative mulch

Mulch is a cover for your soil. You should use compost or straw as soft mulch. But hard mulch can be anything—like the shells you find on the beach!

What to do:

1 After you set up your paints, carefully paint patterns or pictures on your shells.

2 Next let your painted shells dry.

3 Be sure to keep your wet shells in a place out of reach where they won't be touched.

4 When your shells are dry, lay them on the soil in your pots or plot!

You will need:
- A place to paint **(ask an adult** where you can paint)
- Painting smock, or old clothes
- Lots of shells
- Childrens paints (nontoxic)
- Paintbrushes of different sizes
- Jar with water to clean your paintbrushes
- Old newspaper

For more about mulch, see page 35.

Make your own plant labels

Plant labels help tell you which plant is which. They can be lollipop sticks with the plant name written on them, or you can make your own cool and colorful plant labels!

You will need:

- A place to paint (**ask an adult** where you can paint)
- Painting smock, or old clothes
- A plastic bottle
- Wooden skewers
- Thick cardboard (like the lid of a pizza box)
- Childrens glue (nontoxic)
- Childrens paints (nontoxic, waterproof)
- Paintbrushes of different sizes
- Jar with water to rinse your paintbrushes
- Old newspaper

Plant labels help you know your plants from your weeds.

Riley's rosemary

Sarah's sage

Jesse's thyme

Use part of a plastic bottle for an outside label, or use cardboard for an inside label.

What to do:

1. **Ask an adult** to cut the end off a plastic bottle.

2. Trace a circle around the bottle and onto the cardboard.

3. **Ask an adult** to cut out the circle and to stick the skewer into it.

4. Glue the skewer and circle together.

5. Mix your paints. Think about what you want to paint on your label.

6. Carefully paint a pattern or picture onto your plant label.

7. When you have finished, add the plant name to the label and let it dry.

8. Be sure to keep your wet label in a place out of reach where it won't be touched.

9. When your label is dry, stick it in the soil near your plant.

Plastic bottle

JACK'S FERN

JACK'S GARDEN

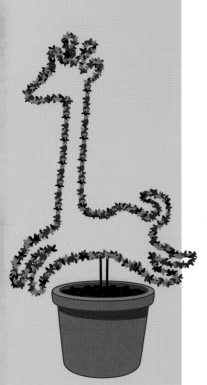

Make your own plant shapes

Have you ever wished that a rocket ship or an unusual animal would come to your garden? Well, now they can. Just grow them!

You will need:

- A picture of the shape you want to make
- Some large pieces of paper
- A magic marker
- A pot filled with soil and two young vines
- Some topiary wire, or a metal coat hanger

What to do:

1 Look at your picture and then draw its shape on a big piece of paper.

2 **Ask an adult** to bend the wire into your shape. They can bend the wire over the piece of paper to get the right shape.

3 **Ask an adult** to plant the two ends of the wire into the soil near the two vine plants.

4 Twist the vines around the wire.

5 As the vines grow, wind the new growth around the wire. Soon all the wire will be covered by your plant!

6 When your plant gets too bushy, **ask an adult** to help you cut it back into shape.

Make your own scarecrow

Birds love fruit. So if you want to grow fruit, here's how to make a scarecrow to keep birds away.

What to do:

1. **Ask an adult** to tie the two sticks into a cross-shape frame using the pantyhose.

2. Dress your scarecrow on the frame.

3. Fill the clothes with stuffing until they are full.

4. Tie the ends of the sleeves and pant legs so the stuffing won't fall out.

5. **Ask an adult** to hammer the wooden frame into the soil of the garden plot.

6. Using magic markers, draw your scarecrow's face on one side of the pillowcase.

7. Fill the pillowcase with stuffing until it is round.

8. **Ask an adult** to help put the pillowcase on top of the frame.

   Use string to tie the bottom of the pillowcase tightly to the stick.

9. Add your scarecrow's hat, and you're finished!

- A couple of pairs of old pantyhose
- Two wooden sticks (one longer than the overalls and one half that size)
- Magic markers
- An old pillowcase
- Some old clothes, like a sweater, a hat, and some overalls
- Lots of stuffing, like straw or dry leaves
- String

You will need:

- Old clothes
- Gardening gloves
- Composting worms called tiger worms or red wrigglers
- Large plastic box with lid
- Four bricks
- Old newspapers
- Kitchen waste
- Garden waste, like lawn clippings, old plants, soil, and manure
- Dry waste, like straw or shredded newspaper
- Watering can full of water

Make your own worm farm

Worm farms, like compost bins, make good food for the garden. But you don't need both. So if you would like thousands of little pets, get ready to build a worm farm!

What to do:

1 **Ask an adult** if you can set up your worm farm.

Next find a shady spot for it.

2 **Ask an adult** to put some holes in the bottom of the box and set the box on four bricks.

3 Soak the newspaper and lay it on the bottom of the box.

Your first full box should sit below the second box.

4 Add garden waste, then kitchen waste, and then your worms! Put the lid on the box.

5 Each time you add waste, cover it with moistened dry waste, like wet newspaper. Be sure to keep the box moist—but not wet!

6 Your worms will help out, too, by adding new worms to the family. When the box is full, add a new box on top and do steps 1 to 5 again.

7 When you want compost, look in the bottom box. If there are worms and scraps on top, move them to the new box. Next dig to the bottom of the box. If the compost is dark and flaky, it's ready!

Don't put these things in your worm farm or compost bin:
- Meat
- Fish
- Bones
- Citrus fruit, onion, or garlic peels
- Dairy products
- Oil
- Glossy magazines
- Diapers
- Dog poo
- Cat litter

Thank you, worms!

Make your own compost bin

Compost is a mixture of garden and food waste. Over time these break down into good food for your soil and plants. It helps plants grow up big and strong!

What to do:

1. **Ask an adult** if you can set up a compost bin. Get the things you need and work out where the bin will go.

2. **Ask an adult** to cut out the bottom of the bin and to make some air holes in the side of the bin.

3. Put your dry waste in the bin, then kitchen waste, and then garden waste. Now water it well and put on the lid.

4. Every time you have kitchen or garden waste, add it to the bin. Always cover the waste with a layer of dry waste and water it well.

5. When your bin is full, mix the compost well. Now it's time to wait!

6. Your compost is ready when all the waste is broken down and the compost is dark and flaky.